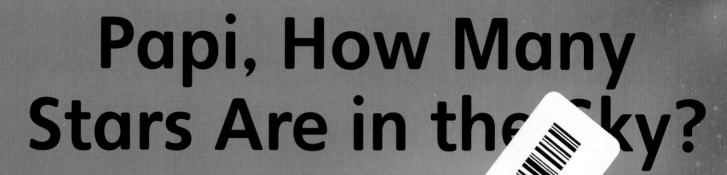

Papi, How Many Stars Are in the Sky?

Written by **Ángel Vigil**

Illustrated by **Aadil Ahmad & M**

TeachingStrategies® · Bethesda, MD

For Teaching Strategies, LLC.
Publisher: Larry Bram
Editorial Director: Hilary Parrish Nelson
VP Curriculum and Assessment: Cate Heroman
Product Manager: Kai-leé Berke
Book Development Team: Sherrie Rudick and Jan Greenberg
Project Manager: Jo A. Wilson

For Q2AMedia
Editorial Director: Bonnie Dobkin
Editor and Curriculum Adviser: Suzanne Barchers
Program Manager: Gayatri Singh
Creative Director: Simmi Sikka
Project Manager: Santosh Vasudevan
Illustrators: Aadil Ahmad & Martin James
Designer: Ritu Chopra

Teaching Strategies, LLC.
Bethesda, MD
www.TeachingStrategies.com

ISBN: 978-1-60617-151-6

Library of Congress Cataloging-in-Publication Data
Vigil, Angel.
 Papi, how many stars are in the sky? / Angel Vigil ; illustrated by Aadil Ahmad & Martin James.
   p. cm.
 ISBN 978-1-60617-151-6
 1. Stars--Juvenile literature. 2. Constellations--Juvenile literature. I. Ahmad, Aadil, ill. II. James, Martin, ill. III. Title.
 QB801.7.V54 2010
 523.8--dc22

                                    2009046756

CPSIA tracking label information:
RR Donnelley, Shenzhen, China
Date of Production: August 2016
Cohort: Batch 5

Printed and bound in China

7 8 9 10	17 16
Printing	Year Printed

Whenever they visited their grandparents'
farm, Ariana, Carlos, and Maria
gathered after dinner to listen to their
grandfather's stories.

On warm nights, they sat out on the porch,
with Grandfather rocking peacefully in
his old wooden rocking chair.

He always waited until dusk to begin.

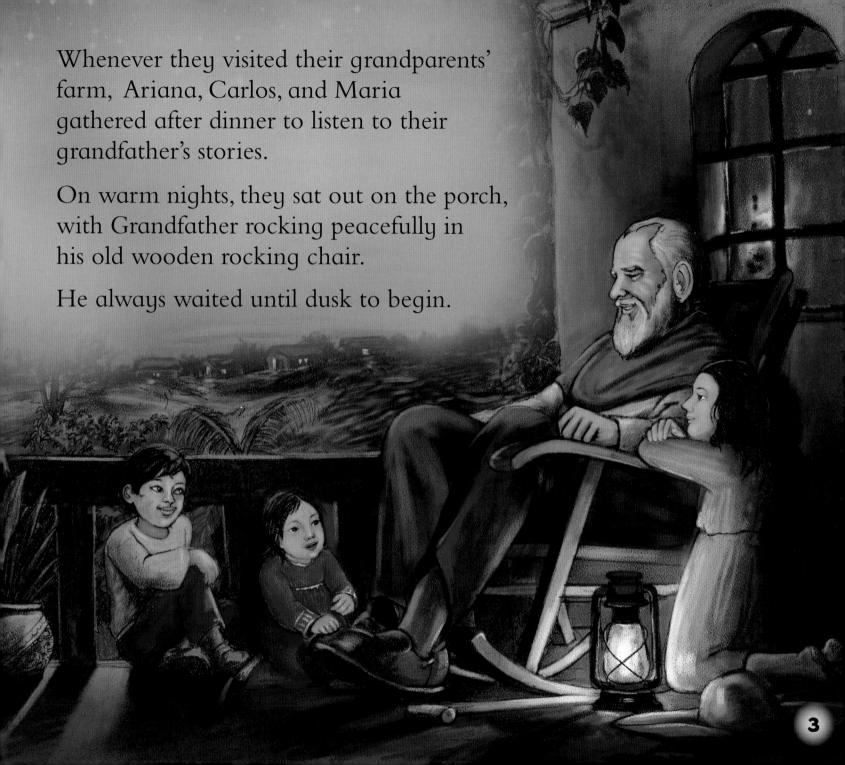

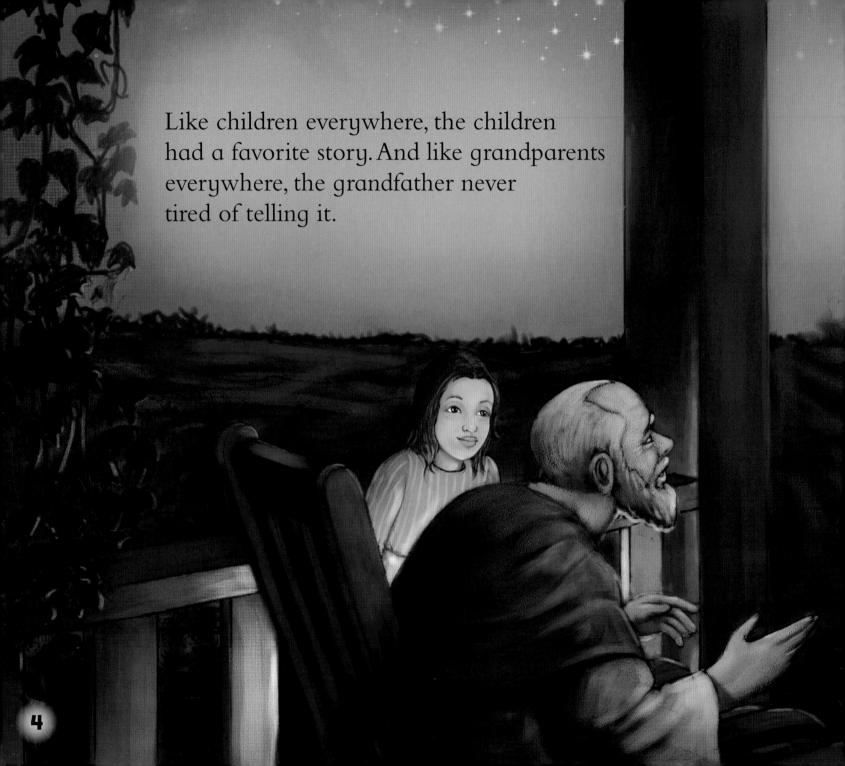

Like children everywhere, the children had a favorite story. And like grandparents everywhere, the grandfather never tired of telling it.

That night was a perfect night for that story. As they looked up at the evening sky, just beginning to fill with its bright, shiny stars, the children began to chant. "*¿Papi, cuántas estrellas hay en el cielo?* Papi, how many stars are in the sky?"

Papi gazed lovingly at each
of his grandchildren and asked
them, "¿*Cuántas piensas tú?*
How many do you think?"

Carlos raised his arms to the starry darkness, saying, "There must be a zillion zillion!"

The grandfather laughed heartily. "Well, *mijo*, that is pretty close. Maybe we'd better count them. But first I have to tell you the story about the stars and why they are in the sky."

And knowing the story was about to begin,
the children pulled themselves even closer
to their grandfather.

Ariana nestled comfortably in his lap,
while the others leaned against his legs.

Just as he had countless times before, Papi gazed up toward the stars and pointed his weathered finger.

"You see, *mijos*, every time a child is born, a new star is added to the sky. And that star shines forever for the child.

That is why there are so many bright, shining stars. Every child is a gift from the universe. And each star tells the story of a child's life."

As they listened, the children dreamily searched the starry sky, imagining all the children in the world. And secretly they tried to find the stars that were theirs, the bright stars telling the stories of their lives.

Their grandfather's soothing voice continued. "If you look around, you can imagine that the stars make pictures. We can tell stories about the pictures. Since tonight is a fall night, we see the fall animals. See, over there is a bear that once chased your father in the forest."

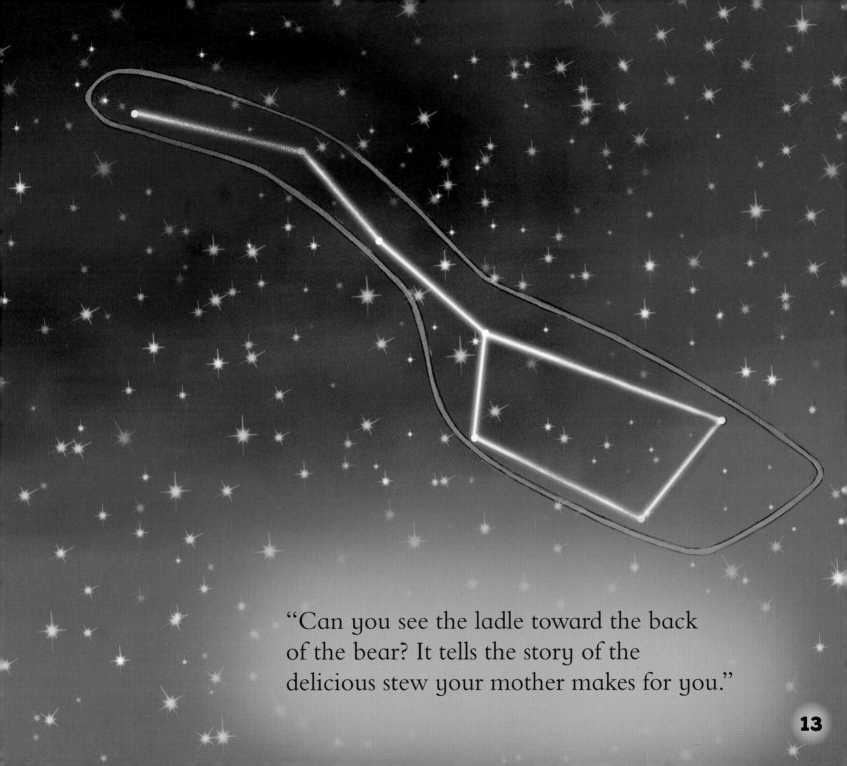

"Can you see the ladle toward the back of the bear? It tells the story of the delicious stew your mother makes for you."

"Over there is a lizard like the one
I once caught at the water pond."

"And through the middle of it all runs the bright starry path of the Milky Way, leading you back home if you ever get lost."

Knowing that their favorite part of the story
was nearing, the children repeated their chorus.
"*¿Papi, cuántas estrellas hay en el cielo?*
Papi, how many stars are in the sky?"

Patiently, the grandfather began. "Well let's count them. Ariana, *cuéntalas*. You count."

Sweet Ariana looked at the sky with steady eyes and proudly proclaimed, "*Hay una. Una.* Look! A big one!"

As the other children smiled, the grandfather lovingly answered, "Yes, Ariana, you are so right. There is one big star in the sky."

"Does anyone else want to count
the stars in the sky?" Papi asked.

Carlos answered, "I'm learning
to count in school. Let me count."

"¡*Una estrella, dos estrellas, tres estrellas, cuatro
estrellas, cinco estrellas, seis estrellas, siete estrellas,
ocho estrellas, nueve estrellas, diez estrellas!*"

With a deep laugh the grandfather said, "Yes, Carlos, there are ten stars in the sky.

But if we keep counting like that, we will never get to bed. Maria, do you want to count?"

Maria counted carefully.
"I see *una, dos, tres, cuatro, cinco*…

One, two, three, four, five, six, seven,
eight, nine, ten, fifteen, twenty,
twenty-five, thirty, thirty-five, forty,
forty-five, fifty…shall I keep counting, Papi?"

24

Chuckling softly, the grandfather said,
"Well, what do you think, children?
Should Maria keep counting?"

But the children knew that their grandfather had finally reached their favorite part. Together, they shouted, "*¡Papi, cuenta tú! ¡Dinos cuántas estrellas hay en el cielo!* Papi, you count! You tell us how many stars are in the sky!"

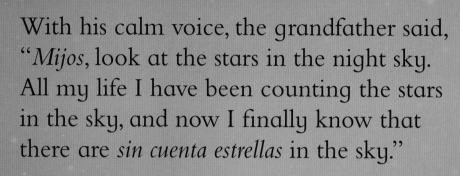

With his calm voice, the grandfather said, "*Mijos*, look at the stars in the night sky. All my life I have been counting the stars in the sky, and now I finally know that there are *sin cuenta estrellas* in the sky."

The children howled with delight. "*¡Cincuenta! ¡Hay más de cincuenta!* Fifty! There are more than fifty!"

And just as he had countless times before, the grandfather shook his head, saying, "No, not the number *cincuenta*, which does mean fifty. But the words *sin cuenta*, which mean *infinity*. That means there are so many stars you can't count them all."

"Your lives are like that, too. There are so many things you can do or be. You can't count them all, just like you can't count all the stars. There are no limits."

As he put his grandchildren to bed, the grandfather sang a lullaby to them.

He sang it in Spanish, just as he had heard it sung when he was a child.

30

Duérmete, mi niño.
Duérmete, solito.
Que cuando despiertes
Te daré atolito.

Duérmete, mi niña.
Duérmete, mi sol.
Duérmete pedazo
De mi corazón.

Later, snugly tucked into their beds, the children thought of their grandfather's story and all the beautiful stars in the sky. As they fell asleep, they dreamed of the many adventures their lives could hold.

Aventuras sin cuenta…